Aperture is my collection of poems that share a common theme –
"life as it is" – serenade, wild, ecstatic; yet soothing.

Aperture is a thin ray of light;
it is the finding of hope in a maze of mystical words.

I picture the images,
I phantom the mind,
I browse the senses,
I feel the tempo of an urge to explode,
I pick up my pen, I write.

That is *Aperture* – life in its natural form.

Aperture
Ovie Ughwanogho, MD.
Buffalo, New York.

In *Aperture*, Oladayo Sanusi, using the power of poetry, captures the interplay of the basic ingredients of life in a way that transfixes the reader in a thrilling spell line after line. Love, lust, family, companionship, the Divine, and nature are interwovenly presented with artistic splendor that surely will enrich the reader's understanding of life.

The universality of gender relationship in love and in lust, in family and in companionship is colorfully presented in poems richly sprinkled with conflicting emotions that bring life and reality to the author's poems. The thrill in a man's heart, the quiver in his voice, the wobbling of his legs and the hesitancy in his decisions as he sorts to capture a woman's love are well presented by the author, who then flips over to present the broken heart and loneliness of failed relationships and life's disappointments.

While celebrating life as the product of love, he pursues life in its transitions from the woman's pelvis to the inevitable six-feet grave, from fetus to cadaver, from youthful innocence to the anger, hunger and emptiness of the senseless pursuits of material acquisitions in a corrupt system of existence. Through his poems, he brings to focus the sharp divide between the lives of the rich and the poor, the north and the south, the industrialized nations and the non-industrialized nations. This he poetically portrays using the river without a boat.

His early childhood in his native Nigeria and the chaotic nature of life in the concept of a disorganized society is manifest in Oladayo Sanusi's poems. Yet his rich cultural heritage shines through. He depicts the certainty of nature and its comforting rhythmic presence. The light, the day; the night, the dark; the sun, the rain. All provide a certain comfort that changeth not. He therefore questions why people rush, knowing that a life built in synchrony with nature is a joyous life of harmonious rhythm.

Finally, the author, armed with an unshakable belief in man's ability to shape his destiny, and using the power of his poetic precision, dances and charges into battle to restore moral order in a world filled with immorality and lacking in righteousness. He fights alone. So it seems.

Those who hunger to enrich their understanding of life and nature will find this collection of poems most valuable.

On *Aperture: A Collection of Poems*
Olubansile Abbas Mimiko, M.D.
Writer and Psychiatrist.

A Physician of the Mind, I have never ceased to wonder what calling makes a healer lay down his stethoscope and scalpel to dip a pen in the inkwell of his soul and give the world with the balm and beauty of the recited word. Is it the unspoken wisdom of The Healer Within that stirs his soothing hand to the intangible but potent, to alleviate the aches of the soul? Is it done in humble acknowledgment of the fact that the aches of the heart find no relief with Aspirin; that the best of bypass operations could not unclog the arteries of the aching soul and that the most potent of dialysis portions cannot cleanse the essence of man? Or is *Aperture* merely a healer's quest to answer the timeless challenge: Physician, heal thyself? Perhaps, a healer, like any other human, is just a traveler on the uncharted terrain of life. And perhaps this effort is simply the gift of a soul generous enough to invite another to travel and discover with him whatever is out there, wherever the road leads.

Whatever his intent, or the lack thereof, Sanusi, with *Aperture: A Collection of Poems,* has succeeded in no mean measure to move the lid to the tunnel that cascades into the deepest labyrinths of the human soul, a task from which most mortals flee. Sanusi's facility with words and sound, as well as his free-flowing style, makes him a joy to read. At once exhilarating and haunting, his verses touch the soul in a way that keep them lingering on long after one has laid down the book. In fact, like any good portion, the work carries the potency to reach deep down and bring about a lasting effect.

From the ebullience of songs, such as "You Are," where he declares with ethereal beauty and purity before a lover, *You are the Glory; I am the Light… You are the Song; I am the Dance,* to an ecstatic outpouring of passion in the consuming presence of his "Treasure: *Say me well to love. Tell her for me. That I have found Ivory. And I have found Gold. Between the water margins. The water margins of her thighs,* Sanusi takes us on a ride on fluffy clouds to the island where love is an everyday celebration.

And just as we begin to settle into the high on love, Sanusi plunges us into emotional turbulence, tugging at our every viscera with haunting wails and whispers like: *I went into the serene darkness of the night…in pains,* in "In Conformity with Light." At times, he all but throws us into free falls and trepidation with urgent, tumbling verses: *Faster and faster. It turned and turned like a whirlwind. Whistling like palm trees. Blowing me cold. Filling me with horror. The Spirit of the dark* nights. *Throwing me back to reminiscence. Making me remember songs Mama sang for me,* in "Songs Mama Sang for Me."

At other times, Sanusi steeps us in melancholic rumination, *On the other side of the river. It's cold. It's lonely. It's tiresome. With no boat to convey home a lost smile…(and) Faces that longed for love rove along dirty streets with tears of boredom,* like "Expression I and II." And when we have reached the breaking point of grief and desperation, and *Wobbled and wobbled towards the diamond shaped dream… The dream that had failed to be born,* with poems like "Morenike," he holds up hope and pulls us back from drowning in our tears with little promises of hope.

Once in a while, Sanusi employs gritty wits to lighten our souls when he delivers laden rhymes such as "Mango," in the originality of an English dialect true to his Nigerian roots. *If man come man must go but make man try to dey come for better places b/cos AIDS dey town dey watch every man wey wan go quick.*

And as soon as he sees a shadow of smile on our faces, he dispels our lingering gloom with the sheer inspiration pouring forth in luminous renditions like "Motunrayo," where we celebrate with him hope, love and humility as he reaches out to wipe a distraught lover's tears with a cloth torn from his own heart: *Your smiles are the maker of rain… Why not let me linger in those smiles forever… Shed your tears on my shoulder… And I don't know when this dream shall be born.* He even ventures to name the possibilities inherent in innocence, *Future and Love,* in "Once upon a Time."

Having traveled these deep labyrinths of the soul with this healer-poet, this poet-healer, I came back still searching for the answer to my question: what makes a healer dip a pen in the inkwell of his soul? Finally, I decided to lay down the burden of interpretation, an enormous task for a physician of the mind, I must confess, and allowed the poet's songs to become me and I became the songs that the poet sang. Afterall, in "Songs of a Poet," the poet had warned: All were gone, with nothing to lean upon. Except for the star that remained in the inside of me: my poetic star.

Merging with "The Passage I" and" Transition I," brought me clarity. In the middle of the seeming disorder all around, I began to hear the soft humming of a stream of orderliness running through. And just like *A mind that was once peaceful with God came into a world of pandemonium to undergo transition—phase by phase. Insatiably. Until it apotheosize to the great beyond…* I began to see the stream fill into a river. And so *With gratitude to Almighty God for giving me the power over my will to rumble and ruminate over nothing…* I found, sparkling in my soul, a pearl that my friend had given me with a single stroke of his genius: *What is amiss is nothing.*"

Aperture:
A Brief Overview of the Central Theme.
By Oluyinka S. Adediji

Aperture is an explosive expression of life. In this debut collection of some forty poems, Oladayo Sanusi explores the raw fabrics of life as he lives it through. *Aperture* is a characteristic work of a young poet with palpable energy and passion. The overall tempo is fast and a vivid use of imagery is predominant. The energy-draining march of this work is compensated by few interspersed soothing songs and sweet supplications, which are factual reflections of the author's appeals and style.

This work evolved from a natural struggle of man with life, not as a means of self-aggrandizement but as the necessary machine to deliver a new creation. Undoubtedly, the author's African background and professional calling brought a characteristic flavor to this collection of poems. The biological energy that produced this work can be felt as I study the pages of this anthology. This is truly a creative work of art.

Harmony, intimacy, love, lust, risks and sex are expressed unapologetically. The opening poem, "You Are," underscores the poet's conviction of the complimentary role of man and woman, solemn appreciation of woman as source of creation and nurture, as well as a safe haven to recline when the battle gets tough, permeates the entire work. This chain reaction started with the mother in the early stage and carried on by successfully developing intimacy with spouse, friends or lovers. The mere physical ritual of sex overshadows the more spiritual fulfillment it entails. - "My Dear," "Tail End," "Mango," "Morenike," "Love," "United We Stand," "Your Love Is," "Motunrayo," and "Treasure."

In "Transition I," reluctance to plunge into the unknown was subtly implied while the bravery and appetite for heroism of a thoroughbred became dominant. The anguish began in "The Passage," but with the consolation of providence and hope in waiting for the appointed time when the supreme command will prevail. The man reminds himself of his immediate past, spiraling to the present, simply to revel in it. He must learn to fish efficiently, otherwise he perishes. The fish tauntingly guided him to the right spot. Risky for both but again the command must pass. - "Once upon a Time."

He is growing and capable of expressing concern, reassuring her that she had nothing to fear. - "My Dear." In the dead of the night when he was weary, he could communicate with the Supreme, his face out of the velvety night sky and his voice coming from the singing birds soothes his aching bones and muscles.

His rejuvenation is guaranteed. - "In Conformity with Light." In his hurried flight, he takes note of immediate threats to his generation. A note of warning he sounds off without chastising any one. A humorous conveyance of a deadly serious situation. One by one, the problems are spotted and hopes offered. - "Mango," "Every Sunday" and Another Day."

His rituals he takes very seriously, appealing to his Supreme commander to come to his rescue. In the heat of his passion, he ventured into the carnal savor of sex as if his indulgence would be tolerated. - "Morenike" and "Treasure."

Suddenly he lapsed into a lighter mood, not deterred by the decay around him. He released a gentle flow of music and he is suddenly cloaked in a prophetic robe. Walking with the Almighty admonishing his people, crying for his beloved land, warning of past bad deeds in an attitude of altruism. His youthful exuberance is revitalized and now tilling the ground and confronting the weeds and the pests. In his haste, he would not lose that which he cherishes as the reward of one does not pay for the other. Some things he is willing to give while some are not negotiable. He has come to know his folks in greater detail and thus is able to work better with them. Patience is creeping into his repertoires and he is able to mobilize his force. He has Love as his pivot and Hope is the driving force. - "Pass It On," "The Unsung Songs," "Expressions I, II," "Indictment of the Past," "Slow Down," "Raindrops," "Love," "Counting My Chickens," "To Wait and Wait," and "United We Stand."

The man has found his own shrine, where without revealing his true self is able to regress to a lower scale. Once again, the temptation of fulfilling the physical needs becomes overwhelming. He takes risks carelessly and more confidently. Hiding behind the wine, careless talk and lavish laughter allows another opportunity to re-possess self. Done as if one now has a choice, at least a say in what is to come. He comes out stronger and again eagerly continues his mission. - "The Blue Corner," "Dry Tears," "Who Knows What?" and "Wobbling Songs."

He has arrived. Now on rampage, under the spell of his imagination, he is transformed into seizures. He no longer trusts the power of his arsenals but believes that the power of eloquence is the ultimate weapon to defeat tyranny. Reaching out to like minds with messianic calls for the formation of a new army in which he does not seek to be a general, but a member, executing the orders of the Supreme. - "Songs of a Poet."

Devotion to loved ones as a compensatory gesture. Realizing how enduring she must have being, he is prepared to admonish her. - "Your Love Is," "To My Beloved," "Motunrayo" and "Reunion."

My time is fast spent and the familiar weariness draws near. He is dying spiritually. The man returns to his root. Back to his mother knowing she can unlock the past and open the door to the ancestors. They come with awe and shock, shaken badly but Mama stood the ground and again he was made to see, much far beyond. His strength he finds again while reestablishing the mother's dominance and reaffirming the permanence of his source. He was galvanized into action, now taking time to appreciate his comrades, living and dead, who have advanced this cause. - "Songs Mama Sang for Me," "The World We Are," "Mixed Feelings" and "Our Hope Shall Never Die."

The man, born again in spirit but still carried the physical expression of his life, presents himself naked. Every body part has a story to tell. He saw the look on their faces, realizing he might have lost the army. He reinvents his mission with a bang of clarion calls. This time unsure of the response. "The Passage II, III, IV, V & VI" and "Our Hope Shall Never Die."

Looking around, no difference could he spot between his men and theirs and suddenly he realized, perhaps while he was in his shrine, something had happened. - "Demons." What is it? The army has been infiltrated and the sacred place has being permanently desecrated by a tumor. All hope is not lost; this tumor can be removed but not without leaving a scar. If that is the entire price to pay, then all hopes are not lost.

APERTURE
A COLLECTION OF POEMS

OLADAYO SANUSI

PublishAmerica
Baltimore

First printing

ISBN: 1-4137-4002-2
PUBLISHED BY PUBLISHAMERICA, LLLP
www.publishamerica.com
Baltimore

Printed in the United States of America

YOU ARE...

You are the Glory; I am the Light
you never walked a step behind.
You are the Eagle; I am the Wings
you never fail to fly high.
You are the Spring; I am the Source
you never fail to water "our" love.
You are the Candle; I am the Light
you never fail to shine your light…
…may your light forever shine.
You are the Wind; I am the Tree
you never fail to turn me on.
You are the Song; I am the Dance
both of us shall always be together.
I see stars of joy in your eyes…
…the happiest moments are when I am…
…with you.
The happiest of all the happies….
…and that is what you are.

TRANSITION I

The red thunder balls of fire sank into the seas and never returned red-eyed.

The esteemed elephant grass has withered and became as lowly as the desert shrub.

The small clever thieves have metamorphosed into kleptomaniacs—
Robbing Peter to pay Paul.

Can man ever be satisfied?
Like Oliver Twist; We all want more.

A mind that was once peaceful with God
came into a world of pandemonium
to undergo transition—
phase by phase.
Insatiably
until it apotheosize to the great beyond.
Heaven or Hell
real or unreal
he transits—
through life and death
with stomach full of hunger
head filled with anger
and the mind uncertain about the transition from one phase to the other.

*   *Transition is a beautiful collection of my poems in a series.*
It is laced with arts, committed to poetry, written in prose.
"Transition I" was written at a stage in my life when I believed that a person could change
his or her destiny

THE PASSAGE I

Rumbling and ruminating over nothing
what is amiss is nothing
life is full of surprises
surprises that lead to nothing.
I have no one in the world
to rumble and ruminate over
nothing to call my own
not even the life that I breathe.
And with nothing for nothing
I go through my life
without a word to my love
with gratitude to Almighty God
for giving me the power over my will
to rumble and ruminate over nothing
not forgetting that there is time for everything.

TAIL END

I am but a poet at the tail end of the world
with so many odds retarding me, for
corruption is the order of my society—
this had made me equally corrupt
with so many ills attached to my name and
so many lies going with my day
I am but a poet at the dirty end of the
world where education is in jeopardy,
politics is at an impasse and my future
remains as a cheat who will rather loot
the people's treachery than sweat under
the single eye of God—The Sun.
For I am an ordinary poet at the tail end
of the world where evils are made to
thrive by men.
With so much on my hands; I lay still at
the mercy of wants…. I find succor in
the glistening face value of gold….
I pray fervently to God for a change of
mind.

Once upon a Time

They both walked into the train, one after the other,
As if they were not together.
Then they took a seat right in my front.
Both were very young.
The girl was young, the boy was young.
Then he placed his arm around her shoulder and
She shrugged him off, only to lean on his thin broad chest;
Both of them did not say a word.

Then she dipped her slim tender fingers into her bag.
She brought out an ointment and rubbed it first on his lips,
Then hers. Both snuggled close to each other. Then they whispered something
and seemed to fall asleep in each other's arms.
They were so young—his face had not a single strand of hair;
her lips were so innocent and pink—they were so young.

If I was requested to guess their age, I would rather choose to
guess their names—is that not more difficult?
The boy's name must be Future; the girl's name must be Love.
The train kept going and I seemed to doze off, just briefly.
I opened my eyes drowsily and they were both gone.
What stop they came off the train, I cannot tell.

*　*Out of the many poems that I have written, "Once upon a Time" was one that I was
overwhelmingly delighted and inspired to put together out of a vivid imagination. It came
at a time in my life when I realized that there was more to love than hugs and kisses; it also
requires the innocence of a young heart, with no worries about what tomorrow will bring.*

My Dear

I heard you cried out your heart last night.
And, I heard the parcel you were expecting
never came.
My dear, how unfortunate life can be
can't you see love in my eyes?
why not dance to my unending affection?
why not feel my glamorous passion?
And let the radiance of my love adorn your day;
let my infinite love shine through
your imagination.
My dear, my love is so intriguing,
it will open you up like a morning
flower receptive to the presence of the
luminary morning sun;
then you and I; only you and I
will form a banner of joy
and all our past sorrows shall sink away
the songs on our lips will be hallelujah
just for your love, my dear....
just for your love.

IN CONFORMITY WITH LIGHT

My stomach pained, my head throbbed,
my chest pained,
there was no one to call;
I went into the serene darkness of
the night… in pains.
The night birds sang a song
I could not understand, in the
serene darkness of the
night I remained… in pains.
The night insects sang a crickety song
that was disturbing to my mind, thevelvety night sky refused to be a
comforter, in the serene darkness of
the night I remained…
in pains.
Then came the luminary morning light, the
morning song birds sang… a song to usher
in a new day… and I woke up in
conformity with light.

MANGO

Mango, mango,
I saw one the other day
someone tell me say e be from the islands
and all my co-workers shared it.
It reminded me of my growing up days when all monkey
tricks have to be played to get those ripe ones (at times
not too ripe) off the trees.
I came to wonder why boys have to climb trees just for the
sake of mangoes.

Just like the name, man go! Man dey come, man dey go.
If man come, man must go. Man dey go, man dey come, only say
sometime he no dey come quick. Ah ah, that time na wen he
go visit butubutu—our town girls, because if you pay
for something wey sweet you must tay to enjoy am small.

Since I come America, I know dey see mangoes, na so so
apples. Does a mango a day keep man from going?
Maybe it keeps the doctors away but for how long?
If man come, man must go but make man try to dey come for
better places b/cos AIDS dey town dey watch every man wey
wan go quick.

* *As a young physician from Nigeria, West Africa, AIDS gives me so much concern. "Mango," written in broken English, came out of a vivid imagination as a warning note to my country people. I have learned over the years to write naturally, as it flows out of my artistic mind. "Mango" was no exception.*

EVERY SUNDAY......

Every Sunday......
I wake up and look through my windows
...I see allays of darkness
I feel emptiness without end
sad faces of people tireless of frustrations
I see victims of circumstancesI see victims of self-affliction
...mothers who denounced their daughters;
fathers whose meanness had cost their names.
...and I;
a lonely man
without a home
without a people
thinks of how safe it is......
...to stand by one's self.

ANOTHER DAY

With tear drops at heaven's doors
I wait,
I perch,
Singing…
glorious songs……
…to the heavenly father……
awaiting… that the heavenly doors…
will open again…
for another chance…
…on another day

MORENIKE

Before her perineum
naked I stood
a poet, leaning on nothing
hoping on God
Preparing earnestly
Praying fervently to the almighty
to salvage my face
to save me from an impending doom.
With my arms folded under my chin
and my brain filled with her thoughts
I wobbled and wobbled
towards the diamond shaped dream
…the dream that had failed…
to be born.
Morenike: Will you be mine today?
or if it is tomorrow…
…let me know.

(A tribute to Christopher Okigbo)

PASS IT ON...

Whispering leaves, quivering in the dark
misty night, creaking and clapping in
solemn voices: God's wonderful gift for
lonely hearts…
…to offer everlasting comfort to lonely
souls……
they listened and listened, someplace,
sometime, a while ago…
all sounds are familiar, life is continued
…as a loner, life is continued in fantasy
In solitude, dreams are made in the day…
just to stay awake at nights, hopeful
insomniacs living a lonely life…
painting the glorious future of life and
death; building a world of strength, money
and power around lonely hearts…
……whispering leaves, quivering in the
nights, creaking and clapping in solemn
voices pass it on to loners…
…to fantasize the spells of life

THE UNSUNG SONGS

Walking along lonely roads with the morning
sun shining across bare faces
…and the unusual morning heat raising
the tempo of excited minds…
…trudging and trekking…
…clutching firmly the evidence of
hard work, looking far ahead in search of a
golden fame; that never came.
Salty sweat running down nose bridges…
…dripping into dry soil….
…singing for the mind,
songs men have failed to sing for a
hard work.

EXPRESSIONS

I

On the other side of the river
It's cold
It's lonely
It's tiresome
With no boat to convey home a lost smile
Hoping for someone to cling to
Looking pitiful
But no one at sight
Fed up! Yet undecided
Time goes only forward
Gradually losing hope, losing the smiles
Resigned tiredly on the other side of the river
Losing another battle of wits.

II

Roving around affectionately
With a penitent expression
In search of "love"
No one to turn to
No one to offer affection
No one to share the expressions
Faces smiling pleadingly
Begging to be taken into a home
To be loved with tender care.
Faces in search of happiness
Faces that longed for company
Faces that longed for love
Roving around dirty streets with tears of boredom
With marks of longing
With hope of triumph
At the end of a lonely journey.

* *This poem, written in 1991, was published in the Guardian newspaper in Nigeria on March 17, 1991. It is one of my many poems that give me inspiration at a time when the economy of my country was at a down turn. Although it never recovered, I keep reading this poem in the hope that some day, some time, some how, the economy will bounce back into stardom, and the lost expressions, the faces of people longing for "home," will be revitalized.*

INDICTMENT OF THE PAST

The past is creeping slowly
Slowly and steadfastly into the present
With a hammer blow on the future
Old distasteful habits,
Errors of yesteryears had refused to let go
It has held on tightly,
So strongly to the present
With a cog in the wheel of the future.

Can the past, the old past
With crumbling foundation
Be really forgotten?

The past is creeping slowly,
Steadfastly into the present
Leading the mind blindly,
Hopelessly,
With bad omen and destabilization
Into the future;
For the "house" has crumbled apart,
Mothers have failed to gather their children,
And they remain scattered all over the world
They are confused and impatient,
They are anxious and worried,
They are wobbling with drunken feet into the uncertain future.

SLOW DOWN

Today will not fly away into tomorrow
It takes us slowly but surely into the other day
Every day is sequential
The day will not just run and take us into the future
Without giving us a chance to see it roll by;
Reeling off with the dexterity of a typewriter ribbon,
Showing us several opportunities to make use of a
Glorious day.
Do not rush
Slow down
Do not rush in haste into the future
Otherwise, you'll find yourself in it empty.

RAINDROPS

In a quiet night
With the serene darkness of the sky
My bed offers me the sleeping comfort
The comfort I used to know
With raindrops on my rooftop
Offering me peace and calmness
Disturbing my dream in a tranquil way
Singing for me songs that saw me through
Fire and water
Singing for me the songs of a valiant.

Raindrops on my rooftop
Reminding me of childhood
Reminding me of several long journeys in the rain
Singing for me songs that make me feel like a baby.

Raindrops on my rooftop
Striking with thunder
Filling me with fear
Singing for me songs mama had failed to sing for me
Singing life for me in a way I could understand
Singing hope for me in a way it cannot be betrayed
Sing,
Sing for me,
Songs that will take me to dreamland.

LOVE

The light of the world is the Sun
The light of the body is the Soul
The light of our life is our Love
Life is done when Love is gone
The Love of our life is our happiness
Don't throw it away
It's our World.

Life is for living
Love is for giving
A loving heart is a forgiving heart
Life blooms where there is Love
A peaceful mind is a seed of Love
Love thrives in all seasons
Love is living
Not only for today
But another lovely day
Love is caring
Love is sharing.

The world is nothing without Love
Love is the machinery of life
A Love that hurts begs another name
Love surpasses sorrows
Love overcomes bad times
Love brings forth another Life.

Counting My Chickens

1,2,3,4, I count my chickens;
My first chicken is big and fat,
Always ambitious to go places.
My second chicken is big and tall
Always inspired by what I don't seem to understand.
My third chicken is always happy,
She seems so much dedicated to live.
My fourth chicken marches like a soldier
Always hopeful to return form a battle.

5,6,7,8, I count my chickens;
My fifth chicken is small and timid
Never patient to sit around.
My sixth chicken is eagled-eyed
Always suspicious of other chickens.
My seventh chicken was very courageous and understanding
Unfortunately, she died in a mishap.
My eighth chicken is plump and robust
Always wasting my feed like a prodigal child.

9,10,11,12, I count my chickens;
My ninth chicken is loving and caring
Always ready to help others.
My tenth chicken is very covetous
Steals feeds from others.
My eleventh chicken is always day dreaming
Fantasizing life most of the time.
My twelfth chicken is never satisfied
Always perturbed and makes me feel like wanting more chickens.

* *The good Lord knows that I want more chickens.*

To Wait and Wait

Eyes anxious and stern
Hope derided of time
Willpower tense with waiting
Waiting for the right time
Waiting patiently like a male frog in search of a chance
A chance to cling to the back of a female lover
Croaking in the grassland beside ponds of water
Praying that his chance may not pass by.

Observation with eagerness
Eyes keen on what is under the veil
Waiting keenly like a kingfisher.

People waiting patiently
With their minds wisely reeling off the day
Reeling off the day like a bat waiting for night time
Waiting patiently for their time
Because the hour is near
The time is come
When geniuses shall be released from bandages
When willpower shall be set free
When dying men shall wait for the cold hands of death
When the moon shall wait for the sun to fulfill its
Luminosity presence of the day
When the art of waiting shall bring forth a fruit of the womb for
all those that are waiting patiently for their time to rise and shine.
Arise!
Arise! and shine my people
For your time has come to shine.

UNITED WE STAND

It is the loving that we share
Day and night we stay together
Body and soul we remain as one
We are united
And we stood.

Like an ant colony
We care and fend for each other
Like a whirlwind
We rocked the weather together
The wind blew
The storm came
It rained
And rained
Yet we could not be separated
We are united
And we stood.

It was like yesterday,
the memories are evergreen in our minds
Oh happy memories
The roads had been hilly
The roads had been thorny
It was as if we could never make it
But with our goals in our minds
With our hearts beating with one pulse
Just like rainbow in the sky
We are united
And we stood together.

THE BLUE CORNER

I sit in the blue corner
Where all faces look familiar
Where we all greet each other like acquaintances
And in brotherhood, we all share the same thoughts.

The blue corner
Where people sit in circles of twos
Yet unified in thoughts
Where cigarette smoke forms a banner above glorious heads
In search of anti-boredom
Where the only music is the chatter and clatter of glasses
And bottles
Where the argument is hot and the audience is attentive
Where everyone discusses their problems
Almost with certainty of finding solutions.

I sit in the blue corner
Where everything is expected to be good as tomorrow
Where the laughter seems endless
Where sorrow and joy seems to merge into one
Where caring about tomorrow is a thing to think about
Only when out of the blue corner.

Dry Tears

Tears as dry as withered leaves searching for water in the depth of the mother earth
Searching for the life that it once knew
Deprived of a source of living in the land of the unknown;
Sincerely and hoping that you'll be accepted this time
Time and time again, you have lost too many times
Sincerely hoping that you'll not get accustomed to being turned back
Sincerely hoping you'll not be denied
Sincerely hoping dry tears will not be shed again for your loss.

Red scarlet across a youthful neck
Black gown adorning a happy mind
Graying hairs on a youthful head.

Sincerely hoping that you'll not be misconceived
Sincerely hoping that your "mother" will not pronounce you a "bastard"
Sincerely hoping you'll see another day.

Death disguised as life
Crawling slowly into a glorified body
Shattering a dream about to be born
Dampening a star about to shine
Setting darkness into a day about to begin.

Sincerely hoping that dry tears will not fill the place of spot
Sincerely hoping that dry tears will not fill the place of ambition.

Things that die before they are made
Poor souls crying for life
Generations devoid of life
Generations devoid of achievements.

Sincerely hoping that dry tears will not be shed for you
Sincerely hoping your hope will remain like a vibrant leaf
Propelled by the cool gentle winds
Watered by mother nature
Forever in love with the glorious sun
Sincerely keeping dry tears away from a flamboyant raindrop
Sincerely giving the energy to fuel life on a glide of high horses
Riding so high to sublime dry tears.

Songs of a Poet

I
Literary inclinations gave birth to the poet in me
Now I perform my rites of passage with artistic precision

II
I see with my keen eyes, I reason with my artistic mind,
I feel with an instinct to make corrections for upliftment of mankind.
I walk in prose,
I leave poetic landmarks on the surface of mother earth,
Poets don't die,
Their work liveth,
On and On,
There is life in poems.

III
In trance,
With rain falling all over me,
Dark,
Thunderous, Stormy,
Dangerous,
I walk,
Holding unto nothing,
But thin air,
Feeling the punches,
The punches of raindrops,
Feeling the thunderous storm,
Hitting my heart like stumps of wood;
And all the stars were gone,
All the stars were gone from the sky,
All were gone, with nothing to lean upon,
Except for the star that remained in the inside of me:
My poetic star. My lone star in the midst of none,
Always there to rekindle my spirit.

IV

Feet as heavy as a mortar
Lifted with the efforts of a bull
Shod in wet sand mixed with clay
Carrying all the burden of existence
All on a lonely head, but smiling
Smiling happily, because the load
The load is lighter when lifted as a poet
Artistic endeavor is the secret of existence
Poetic endurance is the secret behind the smiles.

V

I saw my brothers shot by armed robbers
I saw my people sweating in the hot sun, tilling the ever-hard soil
Tilling the soil for the fruits of labor, hoping that manner would rain again
I saw our women, with babies strapped to their backs, pounding mortars,
Crying out their eyes because cops shoot their seeds
Cops shoot their seeds for protesting against meager and penurious life
Women crying with babies strapped to their backs because their beloved sons
In whom they so much believe are killing themselves over money
While their daughters, the pride of the family, are selling their pride,
Are giving away their virginity over a few coins
And their neighbors are leaving the beloved father's land
Leaving the much beloved father's land for greener pasture in scores.
I saw men in self-made chains
Becoming the servant of his medium of exchange—Money
Becoming the servant of the money that he solely made.
Who shall I trust?
Who shall I tell what I have seen?
I need a confidant, I need a poet to share my feelings, and I need an artistic mind
to confide in.

VI

The mind is troubled
The mind is shaken
Words like fire,
Molded,
With the dexterity of a snake.

Poetic minds are never betrayed,
For they shall look back on their landmarks
And see their artistic footprints.

Eyes like the sun
Burning with poetic fury
Creative thoughts from the bottom of an artistic heart
Brave like war Lords
Words painted like a new coin from the mint
Rolled around in the hands of prodigals
Kept in the warmness of the hands of charlatans and beggars
Kept in the bosom of the greedy and affluent
Daring every thief to take a break and steal.

Let not your mind be troubled
Let it not be troubled, for it is propelled by the gentleness of a
new day
Let not your mind be weary pessimistic for it is truthful.
With a poetic shield in arm
And artistic spear in hand
Let not your mind be burdened
For you shall fight the battle like a poetic valiant
A poetic valiant endorsed words and wits.

Your Love Is...

Your love is a streak of light in a blanket of darkness
A ray of calm in a stormy weather
Respect with kindness nothing can compare with
An inspiration in a battle of wits
Comforting when all hope is lost
Reliable when all have failed
A pace setter in emotional distress
A resounding echo in the wilderness of silence
Music that only my soul can dance to
Understanding when in dispute
The fire that rekindles my spirit
Never leaving me in the hour of need
Soothing when I am alone
Warm to my heart
Pleasing to my eyes
The best thing in my life
And I'll never let go.

WHO KNOWS WHAT?

Something is lurking underneath
Who knows what it is
The sound it makes wakes everyone up
Babies have rejected their mothers' back because of it
Elders have refused to drink Palm wine from calabashes
Yet no one knows what it is.

A thing that has defied the cunning of the youth
A thorn in the eye that baffles unborn children
A prickle in the feet that makes the elephant grass envious
The day as bright as if it would never be surpassed by the dark night
The sky as clear as if it would never cry in raindrops
Children as playful as if there is no tomorrow
Humans as deceitful as if there is no one to account to
The ground as calm as if it would never quake the earth
Bad times as tough as if they would never come to an end
Yet no one knows what this is all about.

TO MY BELOVED

My beloved;
To the tune of your love,
I dance.
To the joy of your heart,
I smile.
With thoughts of you,
I go through this hellish earth;
This earth that doesn't belong to neither of us
But we belong to each other.
From your inspiration,
I became an overcomer.
Worry not, my beloved;
The sorrows of today
Shall come to past.
Our life will be meaningless without ups and downs
We shall hop with the ups and dance with the downs.
I dance all the time to the songs of your smiles,
The unsung songs of your heart
The silent moments of your love
Because you are my beloved.

WOBBLING SONGS

With my hands folded under my chin
I wobbled and wobbled
Because of the news that I am being sought
Sought by my past.

Together with the taper
I got myself drunk
Both of us wobbled
Wobbled like legless gods
On their way to the shrine
To receive offerings of wine.

It cannot be true
That I slept with the new bride
When her groom was snoring
Snoring in slumber
So I wobbled and wobbled
Together with the new bride
To tell her husband
What we have not done.

My wobbling feet
Can sing a song
A song I can dance
Because I am drunk
A song that takes me home
Home to my lonely bed
Where I can sleep
To forget about death
And dream of life
In a wobbling flame.

Wobble, wobble
I go to my home
I saw the king's crown

Outside the palace
Wobble, wobble
I go to my home
I saw the king's wife
Coming for the crown
Covered from top to waist
Naked downward
With royal beads adorning her hips
Wobble, wobble
I beckoned to her.

I got to the door
The door of my home
And she sat down at my door step
Like a queen of the night
A queen indeed
By glory and might
She had a white coat
On a dark blue skirt
With her hair unmade
And scattered on her head
She sat down there, on my door step
Waiting for me
To enter her temple
And worship to her ecstasy
But I wobbled and wobbled
Because I was drunk
Drunk with her love
The love of money
And materialism.
Then a wobbling stranger
Intruded on us
The way he wobbled
I knew he was in love
My queen looked straight
Straight into his eyes
He wobbled hopelessly
Only to enter

Enter into her temple
And found it too hot
Too hot to stay
Too good to leave
And I prayed to God
To spare his life
So that he would not wobble
Wobble to holy places.

I cannot blame the taper
I cannot blame the bride
I cannot forget the king's crown
Nor his wife
I will always live to remember
Remember the stranger
Wobble, wobble
I go to my bed
And dream of life
In a wobbling flame.

SONGS MAMA SANG FOR ME

I
Slowly and slowly,
It crept up like a snail
Reverberating and rolling
Faster and faster
It turned and turned like whirlwind
Whistling like palm trees
Blowing me cold
Filling me with horror
The spirit of the dark nights
Throwing me back to reminiscence
Making me remember songs mama sang for me
Echoing through the nights
In her sweet old voice.

II
Higher and higher
The more I go, the more endless it becomes
The load is so heavy
Troubles are so burdensome
The road is long
The road is thorny
With trouble lying in wait
Sweating profusely
On a hot afternoon
Looking far to the road ahead
Looking into the bright sky
As if asking the almighty God:
Where are my people?
My bosom childhood friends have all gone
I am all alone on this long hilly journey;
My beloved, with whom I made "promises"
My beloved, with whom I made "dreams"
Had broken the promise of till death do us part
And trouble lies in wait

And I am at the mercy of the winds
With mama's songs been my only succor;
With so much trouble lying in wait.

III

Mama's songs are very inspiring
They are memoirs no matter how short
They are armors in times of trouble
They are to share with loving joy
They make the difference between night and day
They fill me with hope and ambition
They feel like the cool gentle breeze, blowing
Blowing with the gentleness of a loving heart.

THE WORLD WE ARE

What world are we?
What makes the world?
What makes a world filled with deceit
Yet we are the world.

The world we are is sinking
With evils ruling the days
And Mischief ruling the nights
Just like it had always been since inception
And always thought to be at an avaricious end
The world we are is without end
And thank God for his little mercies
For there shall always be rain.

MIXED FEELINGS

An old face reminds me of the past
Tells me how much friendship I have made
Tells me how many enemies are lying in wait
Reassures me of the future
I love old faces.

My day was as dull as a night without my love
I am just trying to be fine
Thinking of all the bad times I have had
I fell like a man delivered from the hangman's noose
I am free, I am free,
I am free from a world of trouble.

Sleepy heads everywhere
Eyes yearning for a rest
Eyes crying to the body to take a break
Women looking humble
Men looking wild
Yet sleep will not come
Everyone is about to witness the making of history
Everyone feels like being the hero of the history
Man made history
Man made trouble
Man murdered his rest
Who cares to be part of history
When the body can't even get to rest?
Who cares?

The angelic eyes that brightened my day do not know me
The face I see everywhere I go does not know that I exist
Our eyes met for the first time and she looked away
Seemed to me as if saying, "I never knew you"
Our words coincided and she barked off
Seemed to me as if saying, "I am oblivious of you"
I wish she knew me

I wish she knew that I existed
I wish she could call my name like the name I heard her call the other night
I wish she never asked me that question
I wish she pretended she knew me
Can someone tell her for me?

Because I am penitent
I became like a toddler
A toddler being scolded for spilling a glass of milk
Regrets! Regrets!!
All over me
I came crawling and begging
I am no longer up in arms
Because I am wrong
I am no longer set to ruin our world
Our world of happiness
Don't let us throw it away
It's our world.

Your formalin-perfumed body itches my eyes
Still I bury my nose into every corner of your naked body
Your fixed smile reminds me of the good old days
You lay still allowing me to explore your body
Searching for knowledge with my long forceps
The sharp scalpel makes no difference to you
The pointed forceps do not hurt you
You lay still that your body may be explored to understand God's wonderful feat
You lay still that your body may be used to acquire structural knowledge
That diseases may be prevented from getting to us;
The living greedy beings
You despised us not
You hide not your body
Thank you, Mr. Cadaver, for been so patient.
    (cadaver: medical term for corpse used in the study of human anatomy)

I remember the dark skinny lady
With her face twisted in a forced smile
She sits amongst tattered young kids

She sits amongst them on benches
Benches that are put together by unskilled hands
So dangerous as it may seem
Yet she is hopeful in the black board
On which she imparts knowledge to these kids.
I remember the dark skinny lady
With children around her
Chanting "A-B-C"
As if it was the song that will make heaven to fall with manna again
She educates them from her wealth of little knowledge
She imbibes norms into them
She speaks to them in a language they can understand
She is always happy to be with them.
The skinny dark lady,
Look at what is happening to your own children
All your children are scattered around the world
With one of them playing the role you once played
Sitting amongst children
Imparting knowledge to them
Seeming to be happy
But inwardly sad and tired
Carrying on the task because of his obligation to succeed
Because of his determination to alleviate your sufferings
But one day, yes a day shall come
When all your children shall return
Return to your motherly bosom
And you shall sit amongst them
As you did before with the tattered little ones
And they shall share your mixed feelings
That you may enjoy the fruit of your seeds.

MOTUNRAYO

Motunrayo, my dear
What has happened to you?
Why are you standing and gaping with eyes filled with tears
With eyes like a full moon looking at me like a long forgotten carcass
Why not talk to me
Why not stop making me feel like a desolate fool at the mercy of silence.
Motunrayo, my dear
Your dark complexion radiates love
Your smiles are the makers of rain
Why not let me linger in those smiles forever
Why not!
Why not!!
Let the dimples of your cheeks marveled with your white teeth
Make my day.
You, the child of a lion
You, who goes to the thick jungles bare foot
Without tarrying on your way because you stubbed your left toe—
A bad omen
You, who crosses the big river by paddling with your hands
You, who spell calamity on those that scorn you
How dare you stand like a woman that lost her virginity to a coward?
Motunrayo,
Embrace me,
Speak out your mind to me,
I have a listening ear
Don't allow misunderstandings to become a distance between us
Don't allow lying lips tell us about ourselves.
Motunrayo,
Hold me,
Shed your tears on my shoulders
Let me carry your problems
Because they are mine as well
For I carry you around
And I don't know when this dream shall be born.

TREASURE

The river between
The river that separates
Want and satisfaction
Love and understanding
Runs endlessly as life
Sip out of the river
That runs from the tongue
The tongue of truth
I have found Ivory
I have found Gold
Between the water margins
The water margins
The water margins of her thighs
And I,
A man at the mercy
The mercy of his wants
I have found satisfaction
In the river that flows with contentment
In the river that runs endlessly
Endlessly as life
But cannot take away my Ivory
And will not take away my Gold
I go along the way
I tell everybody
I have found Ivory as white as snow
I have found Gold glistening like diamonds.

The river that separates love
Love and understanding
Has failed to separate us
Because I have found love
Love and understanding
Between her tender breasts
Which cocoon my hope
Between the water margins
The water margins of her thighs

That flows to satisfy
That cools to understand
The river that runs between
The river that separates
Separates life and death
Has brought my pot of luck
Because I persisted
Persisted on its bank.

And I,
A man at the mercy
The mercy of her white probing eyes
Enchanted to the sky
I have found Ivory
I have found Gold
I saw a squirrel
Running along on the other side
With his big hairy tail
Waving me goodbye.
And I,
A happy man
With a big pot of treasure
Requested the squirrel
To say me well
Say me well to love
Tell her for me
That I have found Ivory
And I have found Gold
Between the water margins
The water margins of her thighs.

*	*This poem is one that I was really amazed to write, a couple of my friends made some comments about this poem. One of them wrote – "This is a great poem that flows just like the water margin of her thigh, it is erotic, paradoxically philosophical, sexually edifying. I'll like to meet the lady and discover her treasure myself." Another one wrote this – "This poem is salaciously lustful, I will recommend it to Casanovas the world over. And the final comment by a friend – This piece is truly erotic but vividly describes the writer's worship at a lovers altar."*

THE PASSAGE II

Playing the role of a reversing enzyme
I rejuvenated into the life of a loving heart
Roaring through the thick jungle of promises
Promises that are dreamt together
But never fulfilled together.

THE PASSAGE III

To move forward I need a joker
A joker with the heads of two great kings
Two great kings staring into each other's eyes
Staring with the determination of conquerors
Conquerors who forget that at the end of a two-man battle
The winner is still a loser
A loser who can never recoup the lost time
But keeps moving forward because he holds the joker.

The Passage IV

Like a quadriplegic I sat in limbo
I sniffed the sweet fragrance of the beauty
I felt the intense presence of a redefined glory
It seemed to be real
Yet I allowed the glorious moments
The once-in-a-lifetime moments to slip through my fingers
It seemed to be real
Because it arrived at the door
The door of destiny
The door of destiny of another man
Easy come
Easy go
I wait to find another fate.

The Passage V

Reversal enzymes would not even allow me to move forward
And like a quadriplegic I could not chase after the many beautiful chances
Like a leper I held the joker between my amputated fingers
Despite the bleaching of my skin with infirmities
I am still committed to breathing through my collapsed nose bridge
And the impediments nodules which surround my life
I really don't know my reason for surviving this long.

THE PASSAGE VI

Can you imagine what I am?
Imagine that I have a head
With a feminine hairline
And a biopsied brain
Shooting out in the rear
Like a showcase of arts
And my face——
twisted with time
With an exopthalmic eye
Very indistinguishable from thyrotoxicosis
With my nose like a dungeon for smoke
And my lips shaped like a cigarette butt
Imagine that I have a small body habitus
With a feminine chest but breastless
Except for the rudiment of evolution
Surrounded by tiny little fine hairs
And my tummy slightly protruding
With back curved like a kyphotic old man
So, you can imagine what I am?
My legs are long and slender with tufts of hairs
Like a cottonseed but not as yielding as the white gold
And my feet long and waddling like a duck
Can you imagine what I am?
An imbroglio?
Or a colossus?
Marching immensely through any passage
Canals of birth
Passage of life
Corridors of intelligentsias
Hearts of love
Singing wobbling songs
Along passages of life.
Can you still imagine what I am?

Rubble and Squalor

The rubble and squalor
They litter the roads
The way to their homes
Is blocked by the rubbish they create
No home to go
Nowhere to rest sleepy heads
Except in dust bins
Dark and smelly
Infested with all that can harm humans
Harm humans to the marrow
Yet the rubble and squalor
With skin darkened by the ultraviolet rays of the sun
Lay still among the dirts of the street
Seeming to be happy
Doing their picking of dirts
As if there is nothing in life than dignity in labor.

In the mornings
The rubble and squalor
Sits amongst market women
Who buy their wares off them
Who takes their troubles of storing rubbish
And place them in new abodes
That the rubble and squalor may hunt for more dirts
Blocking the way to their homes
And opening to their minds new channels of happiness
Since the roads to their homes are lonely
The way to their hearts is narrow and long
And happy days are strictly things of the past
For their homes are desolate
The walls are broken
The windows are shattered by anger
The furniture is wrecked by termites
The trees are shrunken and falling
And the home is nothing but rubble and squalor
With the roads blocking the progress of time.

The rubble and squalor
Not seen by their neighbors
Who pass along on their way to the market
With cavities of dirt in their chest
And their blood vessels very much in contact with the environment;
Suppressive are they with several colored chalks
And long needles
Pitied are they by the herbalists—
Who religiously believe in the bark of trees
Alligator peppers and kolanuts, rubble and squalor;
That the workaholic relentless body may work without hindrance
Picking up rubble and squalor that blocks the way to their homes
That garbage the way to their hearts
That replaced a once loving quiet home.

OUR HOPE SHALL NEVER DIE

Something has to change
Our hope should not die
Our children—our future pride; filled with vibrant life;
Filled with innovative energy; to make something change,
Should not suffer—everything should not stay the same.

No time for redundancy
No time for hibernation
No solitude
Reminiscence is disallowed
Pondering is like a pause—
A hole in the spoke of these times we are.

The golden colors cannot even be allowed to stay golden
We have to make them shine
Something will just have to change
Our hope should not die.

REUNION

It was like yesterday since we parted
The cold winds blew us apart because of the search for perfection
Yet no human is perfect.

As I sit here all alone
As I ponder all by myself
Looking back at the flames of yesterday
I hear the songs of your heart
The smoky flame of your choice between loving and pleasures
Yet I don't know why the vacuum of misunderstanding had to be this silent.

Every morning the mirror shows me a reflection of your face
As I look forward to this dream of reunion
As endless as life.

Fibroids

The fate of this bundle of muscle mass is very uncertain
It looks like a whorled flower of vendetta
It is a burden to the mind and soul
A siege of blood to its carriers
Like a pendulum, it swings to cause pains and discomfort
The fate remains uncertain
Maybe it would degenerate with the advent of a new life
Perhaps it would shy away under the scalpel of a skilled hand
No matter what happens to this bundle of uncertainties
Even if it becomes calcified
The old scar is left behind
And shall never be forgotten

DEMONS

So what happens next to the red-eyed man?
With salivary mucus dripping from the angles of his mouth
Like a siege of worms under an attack by anthelmintics
Cannot even confuse the minds of victims
Their bodies are set up in a flame of vengeance
Flames that cannot be quenched by wants
But for this other one standing by the corridor
With legs wide apart and his manhood dripping life from a mortal fountain
Feeding yet another monstrous demon that clamors around to suck lives out of flaming innocent souls, burning their victims with splendid savor of lustful thirst
for blood
Laughing loudly waking people from sleep——
Mortal, mortals,
Unable to return to a restful night
Thinking loudly – so what happens to me?

Printed in the United States
33354LVS00009BA/5